Walking Sadie

OUR NEIGHBORHOOD IN ROSWELL, GEORGIA

Cookie Levine

BOOKLOGIX®
Alpharetta, GA

ISBN: 978-1-6653-0187-9 - Paperback
eISBN: 978-1-6653-0255-5 - eBook

Library of Congress Control Number: 2021914127

Printed in the United States of America   0 8 0 9 2 1

♾This paper meets the requirements of ANSI/NISO Z39.48-1992 (Permanence of Paper)

Author photos by Margery Diamond Photography

To David

and to my grandchildren:
Max, Lev, Jess, Chazzie, Sara Ann, and Rachel,

*Gaga **finally** finished the book.*

CONTENTS

CHAPTER 1

HOW IT ALL BEGAN

Sadie and Cookie: Photo by Margery Diamond

When I first began walking Sadie, an essential part of her training to become a therapy dog, I came home and said things to my husband, David, such as "You're not going to believe this. We ran smack dab into a herd of goats," or "We met a man on a bicycle, and he's a traveling landscape business," or "They're shooting a new movie around the corner."

Unexpected things kept happening, so why not start writing about our morning walks? Call me a dog lover who likes to write or a writer who loves dogs. Either way, it's been fun putting our stories together.

Sadie is our sixty-pound golden retriever with a craving for carrots, apples, and watermelon. We live in Roswell, Georgia, an Atlanta suburb, with an abundance of parks, historic buildings, local restaurants, and a cream-of-the-crop library.

As we strolled our neighborhood, Sadie's obedience skills improved, and our bond strengthened. Best of all, I discovered I don't have to go far and wide to find fascinating people.

Sadie is not crazy about all dogs, but when it comes to people, they are magnificent creatures of every shape and size. Without Sadie, meeting folks would be a quick hello, but she insists we have extended visits.

Our furry friends help us remember not to take ourselves so seriously.

As the joke goes, question to golden retriever: "How many goldens does it take to change a light bulb?"

Dog answers: "That's way too much work. Let's take a walk instead."

Sadie loved her walks, and I did too. Sadie introduced me to a whole new world of people, places, and things.

CHAPTER 2

BEFORE SADIE,
THERE WAS ANNIE

Annie

Annie was our first dog. When she was three months shy of sixteen years, we had to put her to sleep. Is there anything harder to do? It rips out your heart and tears it into jagged pieces.

Annie was my constant companion. We were a pet therapy team with Happy Tails Pet Therapy, visiting schools, hospitals, and retirement homes. For the last five years of her life, we went to Northside Hospital's High-Risk Perinatal Unit, where women were on bed rest to protect their pregnancies.

I watched Annie age, and I always planned to let her go before things got catastrophic, before she peed and pooped in the house and lost her dignity. I hovered over her like a momma hawk circling her young. When she walked away from her food bowl one morning, an *unheard-of* thing, I knew it was time, but I didn't want to let her go.

Annie was there for me a few months earlier, when I had breast-cancer surgery. I couldn't wait to get home from the hospital and bury my hands in her fur.

Losing a devoted animal means losing your best friend, sounding board, and biggest cheerleader.

I discussed weighty issues with Annie during our walks. "What should I do with my life now that I'm getting older? Can I learn to overlook or at least live with my wrinkles, thinning hair, and sagging butt? What's the best way to make up with David for my thoughtless comment?"

She listened to me sing "I Left My Heart in San Francisco" and show tunes from Broadway musicals of the 1950s and 1960s. "Surrey with the Fringe on Top" from *Oklahoma* was our favorite, where the beat of the music matches the horses' clops as horse, surrey, and rider march along. As I sang, Annie and I walked to the same beat.

When I lost Annie, I felt like part of me had been cut off. It was David's first experience losing a loyal dog, and it was tough for him. The house was quiet and disgustingly clean without Annie's hair flying around and landing in the corners, on the carpet, or stuck to my black clothes. I missed a wet nose next to my leg, waiting for a tidbit, as I stood in the kitchen cutting lettuce. I was lonely being home without her, so I purposely stayed gone.

Some days I imagined she poked her head through the bathroom door looking for me, although she never went farther, not liking the sound of a flushing toilet.

When thunderstorms made Annie tremble and pant, I got up in the middle of the night and rolled tennis balls off the coffee table for her to catch. I was not much help.

We tried desensitizing her by going on the porch for short intervals during storms, but it didn't work. I spent sixty dollars for an engineer-designed cape with a metallic lining to block electrical charges, but it did nothing. David and I joked that at least the cape looked cute on her, since it was bright red and had her name monogrammed on it.

As bad as life was without Annie, it had *some* benefits. David and I could be gone without worrying about feeding her. We turned to each other for comfort, which brought us closer. It wasn't enough. Not nearly.

CHAPTER 3

FINDING SADIE

Sadie

We missed Annie's sweet face at the door. We missed the squeaky toy squealing in the middle of the night. We missed muddy paws. We missed assorted pieces of plastic wrap on the floor, the remains of bread spirited away into the bedroom and devoured. After four months of moping, we decided to get another dog.

Adopt a Golden Atlanta, a rescue organization, required an application, a fenced yard, and a home visit. After a representative gave approval, the next step was adoption day. We had identified a couple of dogs (called orphans on the organization's website) that interested us.

David and I were nervous. We agreed the day would be a fact-finding venture to understand the process. No commitments. Nothing serious our first time.

The event was in a huge training facility with space to accommodate twenty to twenty-five orphan dogs and their foster parents, those who agreed to house and care for the dogs until they could be adopted. When we arrived, the place was noisy and crowded.

The organization assigned us an advocate, who guided us through the rooms. We asked each dog's foster parents about the animal's personality, problems, and quirks.

Some dogs were friendly, but others were hunkered down and unresponsive. Several dogs were from Turkey, where they were abandoned and brought back to the United States by Adopt a Golden Atlanta.

Others had physical problems. One sweet pup had trouble walking. She deserved a good home, but I wanted a dog that could hike long distances. Another petite golden looked interesting, but we learned she was part terrier with a hyper personality. Not for us.

We circled the rooms, scratching ears and watching each dog, but I didn't connect with any of them.

When we headed to the last area before the exit, I spied a medium-sized, red retriever standing with her foster parents. Seven or eight people circled her, and the dog was "working the crowd." She was a cutie pie, swishing her back end as she went from one person to another. The dog was having a ball.

My first words were, "Where did *she* come from?"

David said, "I don't remember seeing her on the website."

We figured it out. I always had light-colored goldens, so I didn't pay much attention to the darker ones on the website, but this dog was adorable, a good size, sociable, and apparently unflappable. Since I wanted her to be a therapy dog, personality and temperament were critical.

Her foster parents, Shawn and his wife, Janelle, said her name was Sadie.

"What's her story?" I asked as I ran my hands over the dog's back. Her hair felt coarse and dry, and she didn't have a golden retriever's full coat, perhaps the result of poor nutrition.

Shawn said, "We know she lived in a woman's backyard. The woman's boyfriend didn't like Sadie and insisted they put her on Craigslist. That's when Adopt a Golden Atlanta saw her and rescued her."

"Oh, my gosh," I said. "I would have gotten rid of the boyfriend!"

"You got that right," Shawn said. "When they found her, she had heartworms, so the vet treated her, and now she's fine. We know she was moved around to a few other foster homes before us. The vet thinks she's between two and four."

"How's her personality? What's she like?" I asked.

"She's a sweetheart," Shawn answered. "Very friendly, loves to be petted. The only thing is she's not good on a leash. Janelle tried walking her, and she pulled like crazy."

Heartworm treatment is tough. The dog must stay in a crate for weeks except for going out to potty, which must have been hard on the dog, but she showed no signs of lingering resentment or fear. Pulling on a leash can be overcome with training. Her personality and temperament attracted me. She looked thrilled to be the center of attention, and boy, was she milking it.

I sat on the floor near a back wall and watched Sadie's reactions to various people. One gentleman's wheelchair didn't faze her at all—a good sign, since a therapy dog must be comfortable with medical equipment.

I liked what I saw. Sadie had a squat-looking body, a good size for me. I loved the name Sadie, straight out of "Sadie, Sadie, Married Lady" from the Broadway musical *Funny Girl* with Barbra Streisand. By the size of the crowd around her, others were also captivated.

David wanted the decision to be mine. I was drawn to Sadie, but I told myself it was too soon. There would be other adoption days. This day was supposed to be a *fact-finding* day, not a *dog-finding* day, but I knew Sadie wouldn't be there long.

My gut told me she was the dog for us.

The process worked like this: Those approved for

adoption were to identify three dogs they liked, rate them in order of interest, and write their preferences on a form. At the end of the day, folks from the organization would get together, look at applications and preferences, and match people with dogs.

Our advocate said, "We really encourage everyone to put down three dogs on the list. You might not get Sadie. A lot of other people will be interested in her."

I told her, "Nope. I'm not going to do that. Sadie's the only one I want. It's like picking a husband. There should only be one choice. Who has two backups?"

I wrote down Sadie's name, knowing that if we didn't get her, we'd come back another day.

If the group decided on us, Sadie's foster parents would call within a couple of days. We left in a state of shock. I never imagined that the *last* dog we saw would be the one I connected with. Go figure.

CHAPTER 4

SADIE COMES HOME

Cookie and Sadie

I got a call on Monday.

"Is this Cookie?" a man asked.

"Yes, it is."

"This is Shawn. How are you doing?"

"Just fine," I answered." My heart was pounding. "How about you?"

"I'm great, thanks, and I'm going to make your day," he said. "We're giving Sadie to you and David."

"That's fantastic!" I said. "I can't believe it."

"We're excited for you," he said. "We'd like to bring her over Thursday afternoon, if that's okay, and we can take care of the paperwork then."

"That's fine. What are you bringing besides Sadie?" My stomach felt queasy.

"We have a bag of dog food and a soft toy she likes. That's about it."

"Okay. Just wanted to know if I needed to buy food."

"No way. You'll have plenty. How about I call you around four o'clock before we leave?"

"Sounds good. See you then. And thank you so much."

Oh, my gosh! Nothing was ready. I called David.

"We got her! We got Sadie! Shawn called. They're bringing her Thursday. I can't believe it."

"That's great!" he said. "They're really giving her to *us*?"

"Yes! I've got to get stuff ready. It's a good thing I kept Annie's bowls."

"No, I don't think we should use Annie's bowls. That's not right. Let's get new ones," David said in a firm voice. I could tell he didn't want another dog using Annie's personal bowls, which I had stored, along with her favorite Kong, a hard rubber toy we stuffed with peanut butter.

"Okay, if that's what you want. I'll get new ones."

I headed to the store and bought food and water bowls, a couple of toys, and a bag of treats.

Shawn and Janelle brought Sadie on Thursday. While we signed papers and went through Sadie's medical records, she stayed close to Shawn.

We finished, and they left. It was not pretty. Sadie watched them drive away, and she circled the house, whining like a lost soul. She sprinted back to the front door, inconsolable. The separation was awful for her, and I wondered what we had gotten ourselves into.

We made it through the night. She slept in our bedroom, where she peed once on the carpet, but it was our fault for not taking her out sooner. At least she did not tear up anything.

The next day, Sadie paced from room to room. I was determined to get her out for a walk to burn up some of her anxiety, so I buckled her into Annie's old collar and attached the leash. We made it to the sidewalk, but she was squirmy and had no idea what she was supposed to do. She yanked me from side to side, and it took all my strength to hold on.

A squirrel dashed in front of us, and Sadie took off. Never mind that I was on the end of the leash. I could barely get down the street with the wild and crazy dog.

Was she the same adorable thing I'd seen and wanted? I knew that any rescue dog came with baggage and needed a period of adjustment, but was Sadie too difficult for us to handle? Would we have to take her back?

The pulling continued. I reached out to a trainer at Adopt a Golden Atlanta, and she recommended I get a harness. Rather than attaching Sadie's leash to her collar, the harness went around her body, and the leash attached to the front of her chest, under her head. When I gave a tug, her entire body turned, and I had more control.

The harness helped, but she was still a handful. Sadie was distracted by birds, insects, other dogs, cars, and people. She took off after everything. Our walks were no fun, but I knew she needed to be out and moving. I kept up our walks every morning, and I came home frazzled and exasperated every time.

CHAPTER 5

TEN MONTHS LATER

Cookie and Sadie

Ten months is approximately three hundred days. Except for a few times when I didn't feel well or the weather was stormy, Sadie and I walked every morning.

We took obedience classes, and Sadie learned basic commands, but I wanted her to figure some things out for herself. For example, when Sadie hovered as David and I ate dinner, we ignored her, and she walked away. When we got tired of petting her, we stopped, and she found a toy and occupied herself.

Things got better. After ten months she walked next to me with less pulling and even managed to see a squirrel without taking off (well, usually). As we studied and learned each other's personalities, quirks, and reactions, our relationship grew.

I forgot to mention her coat. In the beginning, Sadie's fur was coarse and skimpy, without a golden retriever's lush feathering. One day I looked down, and her tail was covered with fur. Her coat had softened, and highlights appeared. She was blossoming before our eyes.

Dogs are like people. Like us, give them a safe and secure spot to settle, good nutrition, exercise, and folks who love them, and they look and feel better.

Sadie was pretty before, but now she was ready for the red carpet. On one of our walks, a stranger said, "Your dog is gorgeous! Look at those high-lights. I wish I could get that color at my beauty salon."

I answered, "Thanks. You should have seen her before. Her coat looked terrible. It's taken a while to improve."

Sadie perked up as if to say, "But of course this is really me."

I don't know if it was the dog food, which cost way too much, the multivitamins, lots of affection and less stress, or a combination of everything, but our girl had grown to be a beauty.

CHAPTER 6

THE PLEASURE OF WALKING

A Street in the Neighborhood

Nothing beats listening to birds early in the morning. Hearing them sing is like attending a symphony concert where the musicians come together to make the most glorious sounds.

While Sadie checks out a bush, I look up and see the hardwood trees waving. Tiny black birds fill the branches at the top. There must be hundreds of them. They lift off together, moving in one direction and then curving back like a rhythmic wave. I've never seen anything like it.

Walking is simple. You don't need much—comfy clothes, shoes, a hat, and sunglasses. You can walk anywhere, even down hotel halls at night in a strange city.

I pay attention on our walks. A dumpster is filled with old lumber; someone is remodeling. Denise is walking Ellie, her miniature schnauzer. Roger is in the front yard with his dogs, Junior and Jack. A neighbor has added fencing around his vegetable garden. Guess he has unwelcome deer. Bags of mulch sit next to his trays of yellow flowers. Around the corner I see Lisa with her dog, Ellie.

Joe, who gets up early, is trimming his bushes. We pass Jeff, out for his morning run. Diane walks by with her dog, Penny, a sweet Doberman. Up a steep hill, a new home is under construction. To reach the top, the driveway is curved with switch-backs cut through the mud. What a mess.

A nifty mailbox looks like a boxer dog, with his black and white head sticking up and his legs hang-ing down. These folks trained their two boxers to get the morning paper.

Lest you think our walks are always carefree, I must avoid perils such as red-ant beds, snakes, tur-tles, running deer, and gnawed-off chicken bones slung from car windows.

One morning I heard a weird bark. I turned and saw a red fox with a huge, bushy tail. Not only was she barking, but she also followed us up the hill—strange behavior for a fox in the daytime. I yelled and waved my arms, but she kept coming. A neigh-bor heard the noise and helped chase the animal away. Maybe the fox was protecting her babies close by, but we avoided that street for weeks.

My worst nightmare is a loose dog. Sadie growls, and her hair goes up. If she and the dog get in a dust-up, her leash can get wrapped around my legs, and I might fall. If I see a stray ahead, we turn around and go another way.

Walking with Sadie keeps me "in the moment" and makes my worries smaller. I'm not concerned about what happened yesterday or what *might* happen tomorrow. Taking a break from the chatter in my head is relaxing and refreshing. I guard our walking time in the morning and do not allow anything or anyone to intrude.

Sadie has taught me to forget my list of errands waiting at home. While walking I think of the simple things that bring me joy—a hot shower, a mug of green tea flavored with lemon and jasmine, my soft pillow, a piece of Trader Joe's dark chocolate (an essential), or a container of fresh blueberries from David, along with a hug.

CHAPTER 7

THROUGH SADIE'S EYES (REALLY HER NOSE)

Sadie

D ogs are remarkable. They excel at tracking, search and rescue, and even finding those who have drowned. They can tell when a seizure is coming on, detect cancer in urine, and uncover drugs and explosives. One dog pawed at his owner's chest until she went to the doctor and discovered she had breast cancer.

Dogs are made for smelling. They have more than 300 million olfactory receptors, while humans have only six million.

Sadie considers our walk an elaborate banquet—a buffet of tantalizing smells. If only I could smell what she does. Every day is different, even along the same route. Animals pee and poop, people toss things from cars, and wind rearranges branches and leaves. Others who walk, skate, or roller blade leave their scent.

Thursday mornings are Sadie's favorite, because everyone puts their trash out Wednesday night. Sadie drifts from house to house, examining each recycling container and trash can. Her favorites are pizza boxes, fast-food hamburger wrappings, milk cartons, plastic yogurt containers, and freezer packages.

For Sadie the combination of leftovers must be the Super Bowl of all sniffs. Our Thursday morning walks take longer, but I would never deprive her of the pleasure.

CHAPTER 8

PEDRO

How can a person earn a living with his bicycle?

The first time we spotted Pedro, I stopped in my tracks. Attached to his bicycle were a rake, trimmers, clippers, and a weed eater. He carried a leaf blower on his back. Other garden tools were strapped onto the seat, the handlebars, and the frame with rope and bungee cords. He was a traveling landscape business, like men in the old South who rode by wagon, with pots and pans dangling, selling their wares.

I was mesmerized by the ingenious way he arranged each tool.

He explained, "I work for families in the neighborhood, and I come from my apartment over by the library."

"Wow! That means riding plenty of hills. How do you do it?" I asked.

He smiled and said, "I leave early and take my time, and I walk up the big hills."

I admired his smarts and perseverance. Probably in his sixties, he was a small and wiry guy—an asset for carrying less weight on a bicycle.

We saw Pedro once or twice a week. He was always cheerful and never complained, but one day he sounded a bit glum. I asked what was wrong.

He said, "Oh, I must go back to my home in Mexico. My visa will be expiring soon. I cannot stay."

I answered, "I am so sorry to hear that, Pedro. Isn't there anything you can do?"

He then asked (or may I say *popped)* the question. "Cookie, are you married?"

My face must have fallen to my knees. I realized that if he married a United States citizen, he could stay here. Gently I told him I was married, but I respected his courage (or chutzpah) in exploring the marriage option. We never know until we ask.

I hope Pedro is doing well in Mexico. Sadie and I miss him.

CHAPTER 9

FRED

Fred and Sadie

Sadie's always on the lookout for Fred. In his eighties, slim and in remarkably good shape, Fred is a retired Eastern Airlines pilot. He and his wife, Pat, have lived in Roswell for fifty years.

I'll bet Fred was irresistible in a captain's uniform. His Eastern Airlines sweatshirt reads Pilot's Rules of Flying. One rule is "Joke with the air traffic controller to get a better gate."

Suspended on a pole above Fred's regular mailbox is a second mailbox with the words Air Mail painted on it. Hanging from the second mailbox is an airplane made from a Coke can and metal parts. When the wind blows, the airplane propeller turns and glitters.

Fred has enough stories to fill a lifetime. He told me one about W. D. (Wonder Dog), a mutt who used to hang out at the airport in Greensboro, North Carolina.

"That's right," Fred said. "W. D. used to meet our plane when it arrived in Greensboro. Nobody knew where the dog came from, but he loved being at the airport."

"You mean the dog just stayed at the airport?" I asked.

"He sure did." Fred said. "This was back in the 1970s. As I remember, the dog ended up living there, and all the employees at the airport took care of him. He wasn't in great shape at first. They fed him and took him to the vet if they needed to. The dog met some of the planes after they landed, and the pilots and flight attendants brought food to him. They named him Wonder Dog."

Fred has the only yard in the neighborhood with a stuffed coyote. Because his house sits close to two lakes, pesky geese are a problem, and the coyote scares them off. The creepy animal is crouched over, holding something in its mouth. It took Sadie a while to realize it wasn't coming after her.

Fred and I discuss problems with the airlines when they overbook and need people to give up their seats. He told me, "Years ago when I was flying, an airline employee came onto my plane and waved hundred-dollar bills in the air. He asked for volunteers for two hundred dollars a ticket. That was when a hundred dollars meant something. The passengers jumped at it."

My favorite is his story about Skin Thrasher's Hot Dogs in Anderson, South Carolina. Set in the middle of a falling-down, ramshackle mill village, they serve only hot dogs. It's an institution, like the Varsity in Atlanta. Fred explained, "There's nothing fancy about the place—just a few tables and a counter. There was this college kid who wanted to take his mom there for lunch. When they pulled up to the rundown place, the woman was scared and wouldn't get out of the car. After her son went in and explained the situation to the owner, Mr. Thrasher came out and told the woman no harm would come to her. He said he'd have two security agents escort her in. She accepted his offer, went in, and was introduced to the wife of the current governor of South Carolina, who was enjoying her hot dogs. The security agents were hers."

CHAPTER 10

BRUCE AND BRAD

Bruce and Brad Abercrombie with Sadie

As the sound of riding mowers and the smell of fresh-cut grass float into the house, Sadie springs into action. It doesn't matter that Bruce and Brad (twin brothers) have maintained our yard since she's been with us.

Our sweet pup turns into a guard dog with a menacing bark. She gallops to the front door to ward off imminent threats. Continuing to growl, she high-tails it to the back of the house, to vanquish any intruder.

After the mowers do their job, the next instrument of terror begins its prowl—the weed eater. Squealing and buzzing create a new enemy to be confronted.

Sadie should know Bruce and Brad by now, but I suppose they could be imposters dressed in red shirts, khaki shorts, and baseball caps. She isn't taking any chances.

When all is done, I let her out to see the guys, and it's like a reunion with long-lost cousins. Sadie dashes toward them, tail wagging, so they can rub her all over. Maybe up close she can tell they're the real thing.

Bruce and Brad grew up in our neighborhood. They began caring for a neighbor's yard when they were eleven. Today they have a thriving landscape business, maintaining 120 properties, with a waiting list.

While Sadie isn't crazy about the mowers and blowers, she adores the trailer that is attached to Bruce and Brad's truck. The back ramp, a heavy metal piece dotted with holes, swings to the ground.

Many dogs would be afraid to step on the ramp, but not Sadie. We climb up on the trailer, and she sniffs the wooden floor, the gas cans, and the garden tools that minutes earlier had been her source of irritation. Perhaps there are tempting smells on the equipment, having been used on different yards. High atop the trailer, she looks around like she is queen of the world.

Maneuvering on the metal ramp is good training. A therapy dog must be comfortable on many different surfaces. Once when my dog Annie and I visited a hospital, a new dog on our team refused to walk across the tile floor in the lobby. She was a perky brown and white cocker spaniel. After she bounced through the entrance and her paws touched the tile, she flattened her whole body like a pancake. All four legs stuck straight out and hugged the floor. She refused to budge. Her owner coaxed and pulled her, but she wasn't going anywhere. Nothing worked, and they had to leave.

Thanks to Bruce and Brad, Sadie has good experience walking on their trailer's metal ramp. She should be able to handle any unusual surface she encounters.

CHAPTER 11

DAVE AND BEAR

Dave with Bear and Sadie

D ave and I know little about each other. What matters are our dogs. His Bear is a sweet, older girl with black and gray fur. She's not too sociable, but she tolerates us. That's okay with Sadie, because she's more interested in Dave, with his gentle way of petting and calm voice.

When we see each other on our walks, we discuss our pups' habits and funny ways, as well as remedies for assorted ailments. Bear has skin problems, and Dave has tried one thing after another. I offer suggestions, including the use of Listerine.

Dave says, "I can tell Bear is slowing down. Some days I have to carry her back up the driveway."

"I know what you mean," I answer. "When Annie got older, she couldn't walk far. She'd sit down and wouldn't move."

Those of us who are devoted to our animals understand their limitations as they age. We could all learn a thing or two from them about slowing down, asking for help, and taking things easier as we get older.

Jake was a German shepherd who belonged to our next-door neighbor. After overcoming my fear that he was going to gobble up my children, I came to love Jake, who jogged with me for years. As he got older, he suffered from hip dysplasia. On many occasions he rested in our carport, and I put a heating pad under his bottom. When he slowed down during our jog, he sat by the side of the road and waited while I ran home for the car, drove back, and picked him up.

Since Bear is older, she needs to potty during the night. We've had coyote sightings in the neighborhood, which has made all our neighbors a bit nervous. Just a half block from my home, a rabid coyote bit a man, who somehow held the animal down until the police arrived.

Dave says of the wild dogs, "Oh yeah, I've heard them howling. When I take Bear out, I carry a baseball bat with me."

"I know what you mean. I keep a golf putter next to the back door when Sadie goes out at night. Just in case."

So far, neither Dave nor I have had any coyote encounters, however.

CHAPTER 12

STEVE AND HARLEY

Steve and Harley

Harley, a concrete rabbit, was decked out one day in a Cinco de Mayo outfit, complete with straw hat, sarape, and Mexican castanets. I never knew what he would be wearing though. It could be a fishing outfit, Atlanta Braves gear with a baseball bat, a yellow raincoat for a threatening storm, a Christmas scarf with silver bells and blinking lights, or a University of Georgia football uniform, including a helmet.

One day I asked Steve, "How in the world do you manage to dress Harley every day?" He smiled and said, "I've got way too much time on my hands."

On another day Sadie and I found Harley sitting in a wooden rowboat. I couldn't figure that one out.

Steve happened to be in the yard and said, "Harley is commemorating the establishment of the United States Navy on this day in 1775."

When neighbors walk or drive by, they get a kick out of Harley. Unfortunately Steve had to replace the original after someone stole it.

In addition to dressing rabbits, Steve has another talent. During Christmas, he works as Santa Claus at Lucky's Burger & Brew, a popular restaurant in Roswell, where dogs are welcome on the patio. The owners named the place after their golden retriever, whose pictures adorn the walls.

Steve told me, "Yep. I let my white beard grow long, and I dress up as Santa. I put the dogs in my lap and find out what they want for Christmas." Rest assured that Sadie and I will pay him a visit.

The last time I went to Lucky's was for Annie's retirement party. During our last hospital visit, she did all the right things and snuggled with patients, but I could tell her heart wasn't in it. She lay on the floor between rooms, obviously tired.

After eleven years as a therapy dog, she deserved a rest. Other team members and their dogs came to the party, where we celebrated and toasted Annie, who slept under the table.

Annie remains in my memory, but Sadie and I are now the walkers who look forward to seeing what Harley the rabbit wears next.

CHAPTER 13

DAVID'S GARDEN

David and Peyton

Greens sautéed in olive oil and garlic are something to rave about. "Just stop and pull some," David told me. "Fill up your bag."

It was embarrassing to admit I didn't have the knack for pulling the green leaves. At first I yanked the whole plant out of the ground.

David said, "Wait a minute. Let me show you. What you want to do is break off each leaf close to the plant. That way you leave the plant in the ground."

Because of David's over-the-top green thumb, his garden produces lush vegetables in the best dirt around. "It took time," he said of his rich soil. "I had to keep adding all kinds of compost material to make it fertile."

In the fall and winter, the garden features rows of red and green chard, dark kale, collards, and bright lettuces. On summer mornings, tomatoes, peppers, and beans covered with dew look like a work of art.

Sadie and I pass David's garden often and visit with David and his dog, Peyton, a tiny dachshund who isn't bothered by Sadie's size. The dogs greet each other with competitive stances and low growls. I used to worry that Sadie might hurt Peyton, but the mighty pup holds his own.

Sharing his vegetables makes David happy. He says his garden has been a wonderful outlet for him during the ten years he cared for his father, prior to his death.

We never know what's going on with people. We don't know their struggles or their pain. I like the expression, "Don't measure your insides by anyone else's outsides."

David and his garden remind me that life is hard. It knocks us around with bumps and bruises. Because we can't tell what battles other people are fighting, we should be patient and always be kind.

CHAPTER 14

JAYNE AND BILLY

Jayne with Lily and Brandy

When I began this story, Jayne and her husband, Billy, were grieving the loss of Daisy, their Boston terrier. That brave girl withstood Cushing's disease and congestive heart failure as long as she could, but Jayne and Billy had to put the dog down.

Jayne cruises the neighborhood with her pups Lily and Brandy. Black and white, with petite, pushed-in noses, they are one-fourth the size of Sadie, who considers them toys.

Lily makes it known that she's no threat to Sadie. The little canine flips over on her back and exposes her tummy in a submissive gesture. Sadie smells around and decides there's not much to get excited about. Exactly! Lily made her point.

I knew Billy was a jazz pianist, but I'd never heard him play. He looks like a musician, with shoulder-length white hair pulled together at the back of his neck. I went by their home one day, and the most amazing sounds came billowing out the window. I stopped to listen. The notes took me to another place. They were sweet and sad; they were soulful.

Whenever I feel down, I play music, and my mood brightens. I recently began piano lessons, struggling to learn the notes. Hearing Billy's arrangement made me want to keep practicing. Maybe one day I can play my own jazz.

In the spring a white dove appeared at Jayne and Billy's home. It hung around, so they set up a cage, put out bird food, and listened as it cooed.

The dove never let them touch it, but when Jayne came home from work, it acted happy and danced around in circles—typical male behavior. Although the cage door was kept open, the dove stayed for six months. The following September, he flew away and never returned.

The dove's unusual appearance was a mystery. Is it possible the dove was the spirit of Daisy, Jayne and Billy's beloved dog they had lost? Perhaps the dove came to cheer them and soften their grief.

CHAPTER 15

A MOVIE IS COMING

Not a Movie without Popcorn

A neighbor asked, "Do you know they're going to film a movie around the corner?"

"No kidding," I said. "What's it going to be?"

"I'm not sure," he answered.

A day later we saw two trucks arrive, both big enough to carry tons of circus equipment. Guys scurried back and forth setting up orange cones around thick power cables that ran about a hundred feet up the road that bordered a neighbor's property.

More trucks came the next day, and people hustled into the neighbor's yard carrying strange-looking gear.

"What's going on?" I asked.

"We're setting up for the movie," a guy said as he scratched Sadie's head.

"No kidding," I said. "What's the movie?"

"We're filming *Diary of a Wimpy Kid*," he said, "and we have to put a tall crane in this yard. It's going to hoist a boat up in the air and drop it into their swimming pool."

"Wow! It must take a long time to get all the equipment in the right position," I said.

"Yep," he told me. "But even though it's going to take three or four days to film, when the scene gets to the movie, it'll be about five minutes."

I couldn't believe it.

People were running around yelling out directions and rolling cameras and huge lights across the street. Sadie was delighted with all the commotion, since the entire crew played with her, one crew member at a time.

We watched as they aimed giant spotlights toward the yard and built a privacy fence in front of the neighbor's pool. The following day we saw an enormous crane holding a dangling rowboat. We waited for a while, but we missed seeing the boat drop into the pool.

I asked a crew member, "Don't you need a dog in the movie?"

He answered, "Sorry, Sadie. Wish we could, but not this time."

I told Sadie we'd have to put her acting career on hold, but we would always remember her Hollywood days.

CHAPTER 16

THE GOATS

(Courtesy of Get Your Goat Rentals)

Sadie notices things before I do. We turned a corner on our usual route, and her ears perked up. Small animals filled a neighbor's yard. Were they dogs? Pigs? I couldn't tell. As we got closer, I realized they were goats. Black, white, brown, and all sorts of mixed colors and sizes, the animals had horns and big floppy ears. They were funny-looking and adorable.

A temporary fence surrounded the yard, and inside, with the goats, was a massive white dog lying on the ground. When Sadie and I approached, the dog got up and walked toward us with a threatening look. We didn't go any closer.

I couldn't believe what the goats were doing—devouring every morsel of vines growing up the tall trees, going to town munching. I heard that goats were used to eat a pesky weed here in Georgia called kudzu, but I never saw them in anyone's yard. Sure enough, the ivy was disappearing. Those goats were getting the job done.

Sadie looked perplexed. Never having seen a goat, she didn't know what to make of the bizarre animals. The big dog kept an eye on us until we moved on.

After we got home I poked around and discovered the goats came from Get Your Goat Rentals, owned by Michael and Kristin Swanson. They explain on their website, GetYourGoatRentals.com,

> Goats thrive on poison ivy, poison oak, kudzu, blackberries, nasty vines, and briars. The type of vegetation that ordinarily requires heavy machinery or toxic chemicals to manage… and they leave behind natural fertilizer. Renting goats for clearing is less expensive and less damaging to the landscape. Plus, they're fun to watch!

George and Dudley: two livestock guardians
(Courtesy of Get Your Goat Rentals)

The tough-looking canine we saw with the herd

had a special title of Livestock Guardian Dog (LGD). The company's website says the following:

Did You Know that LGD's...

- Protect the herd from coyotes, stray dogs, snakes, and other predators.
- Work in pairs—one dog patrols the perimeter and one stays with the herd.
- Sleep during the day because they patrol all night.
- Have special coats that keep them cool in the summer, warm in the winter, and dry in the rain and snow.
- Thrive when doing the job they have been bred and trained to do.

CHAPTER 17

ITALIANS IN ROSWELL

The Best of Italy

When Sadie and I walk, we see lots of babies, mostly in pink or purple strollers. I can't resist looking at each little munchkin all bundled up, and Sadie knows that strollers mean dropped Cheerios or cookies hiding in crevices.

We noticed a young couple pushing a stroller. "Good morning," I said. "How are you?"

The young man replied, "We are fine."

I heard an accent but couldn't place it. "Where are you from?" I asked.

"Italy," he said with a big smile.

The woman added, "This is my niece Sophia, and we're taking her for a walk. We are here visiting."

I had been to Italy and was excited to meet them. "Where in Italy are you from?" I asked.

They both said, "Tuscany."

That did it. Who doesn't love Italy, and especially Tuscany? With the rolling hills and seashore, the chewy pasta that melts in your mouth, the garlic, fresh vegetables, and homemade mozzarella? My taste buds were screaming.

He said, "We work at a hotel in Sienna, and we will be here for two months. It will help us improve our English and talk to tourists better."

It seemed to me their English was good compared to my nonexistent Italian. We chatted about

Italy while Sadie nosed around the stroller. Sophia, a dark-haired, olive-skinned beauty, reached out and petted her.

We finally said goodbye, hoping to meet again.

I love traveling. It shakes up my world. By jumping headfirst into another culture and meeting people who speak another language, I'm bombarded with new sounds, smells, and sights.

I've taken unforgettable trips with friends and family, but the most adventurous way to travel is by myself. Traveling alone can be scary. Anything can happen, but being on my own forces me to reach out, talk with folks, and ask for help when I get lost (a frequent occurrence).

Years ago I took off to Poland, a place I'd always wanted to visit. Even though I got mixed up and landed on the wrong train, lost my way in search of a historic cemetery, confused one sign with another, and watched people laugh at my language flubs, it was all worth it.

I discovered how good a hard-boiled egg tastes in homemade rye soup, appreciated the city fountains where folks lingered over lunch, and toured the saddest place of all my travels—a World War II concentration camp. What I know is that I came home wiser.

After meeting the visiting Tuscans in Roswell, perhaps I'll see them in Tuscany one day.

CHAPTER 18

SADIE'S FIRE STATION

Robert Shultz and Craig de Lay with Sadie

The piercing sirens and blinking lights frightened Sadie, but once the guys at the fire station began to pet her, she was sold. Her job was to sniff around the two squeaky-clean fire trucks and inspect the equipment.

The heroic guys at the Roswell Fire Department Number Three Station are trained to handle any emergency, and they even gave Sadie a cup of cold water on a blistering summer day.

On most days that Sadie and I walk past the station, an American flag waves from a tall pole out front. The firemen educated me on the protocol of handling, raising, and lowering the flag, a matter I knew little about. I learned the flag is not raised in the rain.

One advantage of going to the fire station is using the nearby tennis courts. You would think Sadie loves to chase tennis balls, like most retrievers, but she doesn't. I guess she never played with them before we got her. She chases a ball, picks it up, drops it, and walks away.

We do use the fenced-in courts for training, though, since I can remove her leash and let her move freely. We work on heel, sit-stay, down-stay, and come. I want her to follow me as I run around the court—an important lesson. Chasing a dog never works; they just run faster. Better that she chases me.

CHAPTER 19

ROBERT L. REEVES MEMORIAL LAKE

Robert L. Reeves Memorial Lake

In the Land O Lakes subdivision, homes border a lake where a soft mist rises and sparkles early in the morning. Migrating geese and heron rest there, according to the seasons.

It's a quiet place, except for chirping birds and the sound of passing cars on their way to downtown Roswell. Next to the lake is an American flag at the top of a silver pole. In front of the flag is a massive granite rock about three feet in height and width. Recessed in the rock is a weathered bronze plaque with these words:

ROBERT L. REEVES

MEMORIAL

LAKE

1941 – 1968

VIET NAM

GRADUATE U. S. AIR FORCE ACADEMY

CAPT. U. S. ARMY

(THIS IS MY QUEST – TO FOLLOW THAT STAR)

The neighbors came together and placed this memorial next to the lake. As I read the words for the first time, I thought of the heartbroken family that lost their son. When Sadie and I pass the lake, we pause and honor this young man's memory.

It took me a while to remember that the words in parentheses are from the song "The Impossible Dream" from *Man of La Mancha,* a 1965 Broadway play. The story tells of Don Quixote and his bravery in the face of hardship, as he strives toward idealistic and heroic goals.

I like coming to this place. The memorial reminds me of all those who fought to protect our freedoms. It reminds me not to take my fortunate life for granted.

CHAPTER 20

JENNIFER

Jennifer and Sadie

W hen Sadie needs her walk and I'm not around, I call Jennifer.

Born in London, Jennifer lived in Copenhagen and Paris before moving with her family to the United States in 2004. Yes, she has an enchanting English accent.

Dog walking is Jennifer's side gig. Her primary business is Powerhouse Strong. Using her skill as a second-degree black belt in martial arts, she's a personal safety expert and national consultant. She teaches girls and women to be aware of their environment and stay physically, psychologically, and emotionally safe. Jennifer works with corporations, schools, nonprofits, and Girl Scouts USA.

Her brochure states, "The Powerhouse Strong Mission is to educate and empower EVERY girl and woman to live her life to its fullest and reach her goals WITHOUT the fear of a threat to her personal safety."

I know Sadie is safe with Jennifer.

CHAPTER 21

WELLS FARGO BANK

Angela and Sadie

We found an animal lover in Angela Mashburn, Personal Banker 2 and Vice President, at the Wells Fargo Bank in downtown Roswell. She and her husband adopted two Labrador retriever puppies from the same litter and named them John Henry and Jackson.

Angela has a kind face and soft eyes, and she cares for each customer with a congenial, pleasant attitude. She says, "I've been with Wells Fargo for thirty years, and I still enjoy my job." Since technology is creeping into every part of our lives, it is refreshing to meet someone who values face-to-face talking.

When we pull up to the bank building, Sadie bursts out of the back seat. Once inside the bank, she heads straight toward Angela's office. If Angela is alone, she says with a smile, "Well, come on in, Sadie! Glad to see you." She talks to Sadie and rubs her all over.

After seeing Angela, I sit in the reception area and give Sadie a chance to relax. Other customers and employees walk over to visit or give her a treat.

Wells Fargo was Sadie's first place of business. A therapy dog must work in a variety of settings, and the bank, with its unfamiliar voices and folks milling about, is good for training.

When Annie was alive, she and I also visited Wells Fargo. At one time the bank had a special promotion, and customers were invited to complete a form and drop it in a glass jar. The prize was a gift basket. Just for fun, I entered Annie, and she won the prize.

The gift basket, all wrapped in blue cellophane and decorated with curled ribbons, was loaded with goodies—a towel, a water bottle, cookies, and coupons. By the strangest of coincidences, the basket also had a dog biscuit in it. Everyone took a picture with Annie. Although the gift basket was meant for people, Annie became the first dog to win Wells Fargo's customer-relations promotion. Maybe Sadie will get lucky too.

CHAPTER 22

THE HOME DEPOT

Liz and Sadie

Strange-smelling containers of paint and cleansers line the shelves. Appliances sit in neat rows, especially the latest refrigerators. Buzz saws cut through lumber, and lighting fixtures with blinking bulbs dangle from the ceiling. People shuffle their stuff on rolling carts with squeaky wheels.

A hodgepodge of people, noises, equipment, and displays makes The Home Depot an ideal place for training Sadie.

I'm thankful the company allows dogs in the store, and the steady air conditioning and concrete floors are priceless on a sweltering day.

When Sadie and I enter any new place, she's always a little nervous and unsettled. I've learned to stand still with her and wait while she looks around and does a wide visual sweep. After a few minutes, she usually relaxes. Sadie went through this process at The Home Depot our first time there.

One of the cashiers smiled at us, so I took Sadie over. Her name was Liz, and she was delighted. She grabbed a treat from under the cash register, and Sadie must have thought, "Hey Mom, this place isn't so bad." From then on, Sadie and I look for Liz when we visit The Home Depot.

We stroll the many aisles, so Sadie can practice

heeling next to me. With all the commotion, staying focused is not easy.

After Sadie discovered the employees in the paint department keep a box of dog treats under the counter, that section became her favorite. She knows exactly where it is and can lead me there from anywhere in the store.

People stop to pet Sadie, and they tell me stories of their own dogs—some alive, others passed on. Each animal holds a special place in someone's heart.

Our pets keep us healthy through their presence and unconditional affection. I once heard an oncologist from the Mayo Clinic discuss the human-animal bond. He said, "The evidence is overwhelming that our animals positively affect our well-being. The first thing I advise each of my cancer patients to do is get a pet."

As I sit at my computer, Sadie lies on her sofa a few feet away, her head on the armrest, watching me. If I leave to grab a cup of tea or take a potty break, she's with me. If I go toward the kitchen, her beloved room, she's with me. If I head out to get the mail, she's at the door when I return. Knowing she's close by, ready to follow me anywhere, makes me happy.

When I listen to strangers in The Home Depot

share their memories of a devoted pet and watch their faces soften, I understand the profound effect animals have on our lives.

CHAPTER 23

THE ROSWELL NURSING AND REHABILITATION CENTER

The Roswell Nursing and Rehabilitation Center

The Roswell Nursing and Rehabilitation Center has been on Green Street for fifty years, while everything around it has changed. Nearby are hair salons, restaurants with outdoor seating, an art gallery, and a synagogue.

Greenwoods and Swallow at the Hollow, two popular restaurants close by, both owned by the same person and known for their fried chicken, barbeque, pies, and unsurpassed chocolate-chip banana pudding, recently closed.

The Roswell Nursing and Rehabilitation Center is a red brick building that doesn't look big, but it is. With two floors, the facility's capacity is 268 residents, and the staff provides long-term care, short-term rehabilitation, and treatment for dementia.

On a nice day folks sit outside in rocking chairs or wheelchairs on the porch, which is bordered by yellow and purple pansies.

When Sadie and I walked down Green Street for the first time, Sadie's ears perked up. We got closer, and she went straight toward an auburn-haired woman in a wheelchair.

"Is it okay for her to come over?" I asked.

"Of course," she answered. "I'd love to see her. I've had so many dogs of my own, but I don't have one now. What's her name?"

"It's Sadie," I answered.

The woman broke into a big smile.

Not bothered at all by the wheelchair, Sadie put her head in the woman's lap.

"I remember years ago," the woman said wistfully, "I had lots of dogs, and I trained them myself. It was hard work, but it was so much fun. We even competed at dog shows."

Sadie's head was still in her lap.

"That must have been great," I answered. "How are you doing?"

"I'm okay," she said, "but I've got to have surgery and then rehab."

She seemed in good spirits, but I didn't want to wear her out by staying too long. "Would you like us to come back?" I asked.

"Absolutely!" She gave me her name and room number.

A week later, we returned. After signing in and getting directions, we started down the hall, crowded with people and staff members pushing carts with medical equipment. Sadie was distracted by all the turmoil, but she stayed with me. When we got to the room, the door was partially closed.

"Hello? I'm here with my dog Sadie," I said. "Would you like some company?"

"Oh, yes," she said in a strong voice. "Come on in."

We walked around a food tray, an IV apparatus, and tangled cords.

The woman said, "I told my daughter about you and Sadie. I'm so glad to see you."

Sadie remembered the woman and went to the bed to be petted.

After chatting a while, we left. I was proud of Sadie. Although she was not yet certified, I knew she had the skills and intuition to be a great therapy dog.

Amazing things can happen during a therapy visit. Earlier I had taken Annie to a children's rehabilitation center and watched as a therapist tried to get a young girl to jump over a long pole on the floor. The child of about five or six refused, adamant that she wasn't going to do it.

I watched several attempts and decided to take Annie over. I said to the child, "Well, if Annie jumps over the pole first, will you do it?"

The child crossed her arms, puckered her lips, and said nothing.

Annie and I walked to the pole. I gave her a signal to jump, and she did it like a champ. Everybody clapped and cheered.

"Okay, now it's your turn," I said to the child. "Show Annie you can do it. She's going to watch."

The child looked away, walked slowly to the pole, paused for a second, and then jumped. Another round of cheers and clapping. Modeling a dog's behavior works!

Maybe one day Sadie and I will return to the Roswell Nursing and Rehabilitation Center. Patients in their program could strengthen their arm and shoulder muscles by petting Sadie and brushing her coat. Sadie would be all in for it.

CHAPTER 24

CANTON STREET

Cookie and Sadie with Travis Tivwell, a server at the 1920 Tavern

C anton Street, in the heart of Roswell's Historic District, entices people from all over. Wooden benches, muted gaslights, and seasonal flowers run the length of the street. After Sadie and I walk all the way to Canton Street, an ideal spot to people watch and dog watch, we locate a bench and rest.

At the restaurants that line Canton Street, you can find all types of food, from ceviche to sweet-potato tacos. The Fickle Pickle is a popular lunch spot showcasing cream cheese brownies and crispy fried pickles. Behind a Pilates studio is The Pie Hole, well worth a visit.

Along the way, stores sell fragrant oils and zesty vinegars, kayaks, and outdoor activewear, holistic pet foods, and boutique clothing.

Therapists have offices in an old home with rocking chairs out front. The owner of a financial services company renovated an original home but kept the handsome, exterior stone. The Cat Clinic is there, as well as a home goods/design store. Next to a beauty salon and spa are business offices and a yoga studio.

A stroll down the side streets off Canton reveals pricey new developments as well as restored older homes. Apartments are going up on the corner of Canton Street and Woodstock Road.

We enjoy talking to folks and noticing construction changes, like watching a crew transform an older home into a trendy coffee shop. The added curved brick walkway reminds me of the yellow brick road from *The Wizard of Oz*.

A hidden treasure sits in front of a private home. A small bowl with a tiny pipe hovering over it has a sign that reads Step On Me. I press a metal bar, and fresh water flows into the bowl. Sadie goes straight for it and drinks her fill. The owners turn the water off in cold weather, to avoid freezing, but they rig it up again for the summer.

While Sadie and I walk, I can tell when someone wants to interact with her. A young man with a huge grin walked toward us.

"What a great dog!" he said. "Can I pet her? What's her name?"

"Of course, you can. Her name is Sadie," I answered. We sat together on a low stone wall while he scratched behind her ears. "She sure likes you," I said. "Do you work around here?"

"I do," he said. "I'm a bartender at the Nineteen Twenty Tavern."

"I've heard good things about the place. Maybe my husband and I will try it."

"You won't be disappointed," he said.

"She's so pretty." He ran his hands over Sadie's coat. "She reminds me of my dog."

"Do you have pictures?" I asked.

"Sure do." He pulled out his phone and showed me. He told me about his dog's funny habits and adventures they had shared.

After a while we both walked on. What I love about these unexpected encounters is listening to other people's stories about their beloved pets. Two strangers and a dog can make magic, and the magical setting of Canton Street adds the finishing touch.

THE DAY I ALMOST LOST HER

Island Ford Chattahoochee River National Recreation Area

On a chilly fall morning, I bundled up and took Sadie to Island Ford Park by the Chattahoochee River. I'd hiked there for years with Annie.

The entrance to the park led the car through dense woods. The trees were filled with leaves, changing to yellows and reds. A deer lingered in the road, taking his time to cross. I drove around a small lake where parents take their kids to fish.

After a mile or so I pulled up to the parking lot and Ranger Station—an authentic log cabin built in the 1940s as a summer home for Atlantans.

I stuck my senior pass on the dashboard, grabbed my gear, and got out. Sadie's tail went up as she flitted around, lured by new smells.

We meandered down a curving walkway toward the river. The sight of the fast-moving water took my breath away. Light rippled with blues and greens, while floating geese dunked their heads in search of food. The air smelled clean. As we scampered the rest of the way, Sadie investigated and sniffed the ground.

Without people or cars, the area was whisper quiet. The only sounds were the rushing water and chirping birds. I welcomed the serenity and didn't utter a word.

The walking path along the river bulged with stones and rocks. I saw fishermen outfitted in high rubber pants and standing in the middle of the river. As they cast their lines, the rapid current swished around them.

Sadie and I passed a secluded cove, where I had once seen two white swans.

Farther down the trail, enormous rocks jutted out of the water, and I watched the geese play a game. They swam to a spot and waited for the moving current to carry them over the rocks. After drifting down river, they returned to do it over again.

Along the trail were two gigantic rock outcroppings, perfect shelter for the Native Americans who inhabited the area long ago. One had a deep shelf with an overhang, an ideal shield from the weather. I had seen curious children, hiking with their families, scramble to the top of the rocks before their nervous parents yelled for them to get down.

When the river trail ended, we turned left toward a steep hill with switchbacks cut into the dirt. When Annie was with me, I removed her leash in this secluded area, and she stayed close. I decided to try it with Sadie. I unhooked her leash, and off we went.

Not ten seconds later, the biggest deer I ever saw

bolted out of the trees. Sadie took off like a race-horse. I watched as the galloping deer flew over a ridge and disappeared with Sadie right behind.

I screamed the words I taught her, "Sadie, come, come, come!" I called again and again, but she was gone. I imagined her chasing the deer for miles and ending up in a strange place or hit by a car and killed.

I didn't know what to do. She had a microchip and tag, but those things wouldn't save her from getting hit.

Feeling helpless, I kept calling until my throat was raw. She had run in the direction of the parking lot, so I headed back to the car. Sprinting down the hill, I kept calling her.

Several hikers passed me. Close to tears, I slowed down and blurted out, "I've lost my dog! She went after a deer. I don't know what to do."

"What does she look like? What's her name?" a hiker asked.

"She's dark red, about sixty pounds. Her name's Sadie."

"We'll look for her," he answered. "If we see her, we'll hold on to her."

I thanked them and hurried off, feeling guilty and stupid for letting her off leash. Chances were good I would never see her again.

I kept screaming for her, but no Sadie. About fifteen minutes later, one of the hikers I'd seen caught up with me.

"We've got her," he said. "My wife's holding her. C'mon!" I ran back up the hill with him.

"There they are," he said.

His wife was standing next to Sadie, who was sitting calmly, oblivious to the aggravation she had caused.

I was relieved and ready to strangle her at the same time. "Oh, my gosh! I thought I'd never see her again. How can I ever thank you?" I panted, out of breath.

The woman said, "Oh, we're just happy we saw her. The funniest thing is that she was sitting on the trail, quiet as could be, just looking around. She didn't try to run away or anything. She sure is friendly. And this nice man gave me his belt to loop around her neck so I could hold her."

I caught my breath, thanked them again, and hugged everybody.

After they left, I realized Sadie had backtracked to the exact location where she had taken off.

I learned that hunting/retrieving dogs who run off in search of birds or animals find their way back to the same spot. Some dog owners leave a sweater or an open crate to await the dog's return. If I'd known, I would have stayed put.

Sadie will not be off leash again. My gray hairs multiplied tenfold that day, but all ended well. I assume the deer made a safe escape.

CHAPTER 26

SADIE'S FIRST THANKSGIVING

(Photo by Ilana Katz)
Back row left to right: John Grosshandler, Harris Fogel, Andrea
Cushing, Allie Fogel, Aaron Rosenberg, Kerri Fogel, Stacye Fogel,
Jay Bernath, Sara Ann Levine, Rachel Levine, David Perling, Lev
Grosshandler, Kenneth Levine, Jess Grosshandler
Middle row left to right: Paula Levine, Stacy Levine, Sandra
Stringfellow, Val Poehlein, Sadie, Max Grosshandler
Front row left to right: Sybil Bernath, Sheryl Erez, Melanie Levine,
Jennifer Levine Grosshandler, Chazzie Grosshandler, Cookie Levine

I n 2018, we had a noisy crowd for Sadie's first Thanksgiving.

Folks came carrying bowls of roasted veggies, a platter of sweet potatoes drizzled with pecans and coconut, a huge pan of mashed potatoes, an ice-cream turkey cake from Baskin-Robbins, and chocolate marshmallow cookies shaped like Pilgrim hats.

Sadie assumed her role as ferocious watchdog. She kept barking until she realized that each human smelled delightful and was a potential source of treats.

As we hunkered down and demolished the food, Sadie roamed the kitchen searching for tidbits. After lunch we took a family picture on the deck. Look closely, and you will see Sadie. She was a hit.

CHAPTER 27

SHE DID IT

Cookie and Sadie, Photo by Margery Diamond

We arrived at the site for the Happy Tails Pet Therapy certification test and entered a large building with an open area divided in sections for testing stations. People were talking and milling about, and dogs were taking turns as they moved through the tests.

The stations were designed to simulate conditions likely to occur during visits to facilities. Sadie's performance on the tests would show whether she had the temperament and behavior to be a therapy dog and how the two of us worked as a team.

"Hi. Come on over," a woman said. "Let's get you signed in. Then you can wait over there, and somebody will call you when they're ready."

We waited. I breathed slowly to stay calm, knowing that Sadie would detect any nervousness on my part.

Eventually a woman walked over to us and said, "Hi, you must be Cookie and Sadie."

I nodded.

Ready to get started?"

"Yes, we're ready." I answered.

"C'mon with me to the first station."

We followed her.

"Well, look at you, Sadie. What a pretty girl," she said as she petted her, brushed her, and checked out her body. The woman grabbed a walking cane and asked me to approach her with Sadie, who sniffed the cane, but otherwise showed no interest.

"Good girl," I said to Sadie as we moved to the next station—obedience skills.

"Hey there," a guy said as I handed him our evaluation form.

"First I want to see how she heels with you, so walk her around the orange cones in the direction of the arrows. Just weave around them."

"Sadie, watch," I said.

She looked straight at me.

"Sadie, heel." We took off and maneuvered around the cones.

"Okay, put her in a sit-stay and walk away to the orange line on the floor. I'll let you know when thirty seconds are up. Then walk back to her side and release her."

"Sadie, sit, please," I said.

Sadie looked at me and put her bottom down.

"Stay," I said in a firm voice. I walked to the line, turned around to face her, and waited until the guy told me to return.

"Free!" I said, and she got up. "Good girl!"

"Now put her in a down-stay," he said. "Walk to the line again, and when time is up, I want you to call her to you."

"Sadie, down, please," I said. I pointed at the floor. She did it.

"Stay." I walked to the line and waited. When time was up, I crouched down, opened my arms wide, and said in a cheerful voice, "Sadie, come!"

Sadie jumped up and bounded into my arms.

"Good girl!"

The next station tested Sadie's ability to stay calm around another dog. We walked toward a person with his dog. When we got close, I paused and chatted with the other owner as Sadie stayed by my side.

At the following station, we approached two people, one in a wheelchair and another using a walker. Sadie was fine, just nosey. The evaluators watched her reaction as someone opened an umbrella in front of her, dropped a book and a metal plate on the floor, scooted past her with another dog, and ran by her wearing a big hat with bells and tassels. Sadie was surprised, but she didn't panic.

After these distractions, four evaluators came over and hugged Sadie at the same time, a frequent happening on a visit to a children's facility. She ate it up.

"So, Cookie," the evaluator said, "We want you to go into the office and leave Sadie with us for three minutes. We'll come get you."

I knew what this final test was about. If we were at a facility and I had to hand Sadie off in an emergency or for any reason, Sadie would have to tolerate being away from me.

I went to the office and waited, fidgeting. When the time was up, they brought Sadie in with a red Happy Tails bandana tied around her neck. She passed! After congratulations and hugs, someone took a picture for our official badge.

As soon as we got to the car, I called David.

"She did it! She was fantastic! She passed everything."

"That's great," David said. "I knew she could do it."

We were excited and relieved. On the way home, I thought of all the days over the previous two and one-half years I had worked with Sadie, doing obedience training, exercising her, and building a relationship. I thought of David's unlimited patience that helped her get acclimated and the countless hours of petting.

We took in a fearful, untrained, and insecure "wild child" and helped her become a great dog. Sadie is calmer, more trusting, and happier than when she first came to us, and she will get even better over time.

She is beginning her career as a certified therapy

dog. We have volunteered with the Weinstein Hospice, cheered up surgical patients at Northside Hospital, and visited residents at The Cohen Home, an assisted living and dementia care community, where Sadie struts around and shares her inimitable charm.

Walking with Sadie opened my eyes and showed me how much there is to see if I watch and listen, if I get out of my own head, if I attend to the present moment. My mornings became adventures. What new object would I notice? Who would I meet? What would I learn?

Whatever David and I did for Sadie will never measure up to what she's done for us. We know she won't be with us long enough, and we know our hearts will break when she's gone. We signed up for everything when she came, though, and we wouldn't want to miss a minute.

ACKNOWLEDGMENTS

Many thanks to early readers of the manuscript: Cathy Maher, Fran Rothenberg, and Ron Skinner. Thank you to Helen Kelly for reading a portion of the manuscript and for referring me to Bobbie Christmas, editor and owner of Zebra Communications. Bobbie, your expertise and suggestions made this book so much better. I can't wait to work with you again. To the team at BookLogix, thank you for patiently guiding me through the world of publishing. Immeasurable thanks to photographer, Margery Diamond, for all your help and for a wonderful cover photo, despite a moving dog.

Special thanks to my neighbors for our interesting, enjoyable encounters and for kindly allowing me to include you in my book. To my delightful neighbors who are not in the book, my sincere apologies. I had to stop somewhere.

Most of all, thank you to my husband, David, for your enduring support and steady presence. You are my rock in this crazy world.

Five generations of the Levine family's golden retrievers began with Heather, followed by Candy, Tammy, Nike, and Tiffany. Memories of our dogs are with me to this day. They were the best part of our family. They licked away our tears, knocked everything off the tables, and taught us the meaning of fun.

When our first dog, Heather, died, I wrote this:

"We'll never forget you as long as we live,
For joy and happiness to us you did give."

ABOUT THE AUTHOR

Photo by Margery Diamond

Cookie Levine lives with her husband, David, and Sadie, their golden retriever, in Roswell, Georgia. After a long career as a lawyer, mediator, and arbitrator, Cookie earned a masters in professional writing from Kennesaw State University. She has written about the best time of her day—walking Sadie.

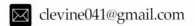 clevine041@gmail.com